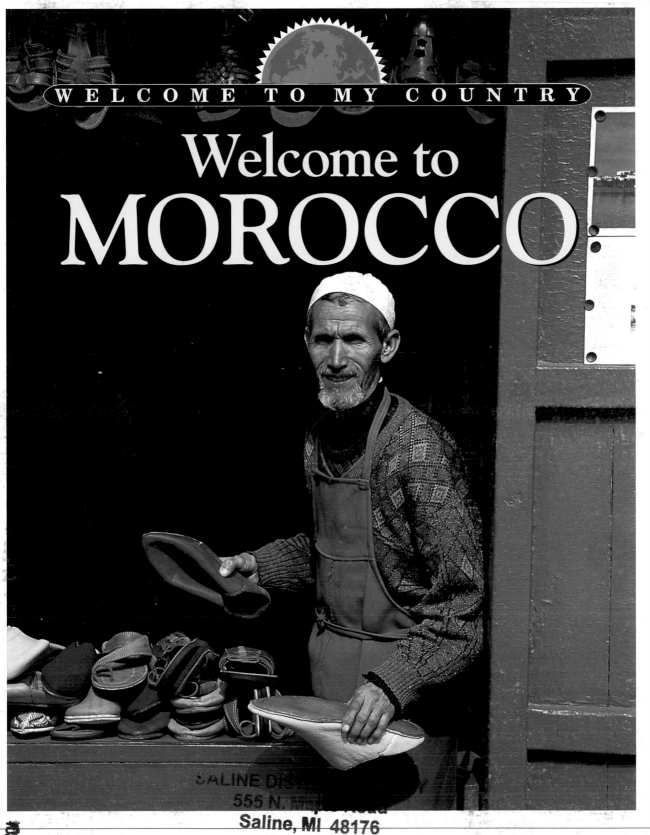

W9-BNC-530

WELCOME TO MY COUNTRY

Welcome to
MOROCCO

SALINE DI...
555 N. Maple Road
Saline, MI 48176

Gareth Stevens Publishing
A WORLD ALMANAC EDUCATION GROUP COMPANY

Written by
DEBORAH FORDYCE

Edited by
MELVIN NEO

Edited in USA by
DOROTHY L. GIBBS

Designed by
GEOSLYN LIM

Picture research by
SUSAN JANE MANUEL

First published in North America in 2004 by
Gareth Stevens Publishing
A World Almanac Education Group Company
330 West Olive Street, Suite 100
Milwaukee, Wisconsin 53212 USA

Please visit our web site at:
www.garethstevens.com
For a free color catalog describing
Gareth Stevens Publishing's list of high-quality
books and multimedia programs,
call 1-800-542-2595 (USA) or
1-800-387-3178 (Canada).
Gareth Stevens Publishing's fax: (414) 332-3567.

© **TIMES MEDIA PRIVATE LIMITED 2004**
Originated and designed by
Times Editions
An imprint of Times Media Private Limited
A member of the Times Publishing Group
Times Centre, 1 New Industrial Road
Singapore 536196
http://www.timesone.com.sg/te

Library of Congress Cataloging-in-Publication Data
Fordyce, Deborah.
Welcome to Morocco / Deborah Fordyce.
p. cm. — (Welcome to my country)
Summary: An overview of the geography, history,
government, economy, people, and culture of Morocco.
Includes bibliographical references and index.
ISBN 0-8368-2561-6 (lib. bdg.)
1. Morocco—Juvenile literature. [1. Morocco.]
I. Title. II. Series.
DT305.F67   2004
964—dc22   2003061097

Printed in Singapore

1 2 3 4 5 6 7 8 9 08 07 06 05 04

PICTURE CREDITS
ANA Press Agency: 3 (center), 11, 26,
    30 (bottom), 32 (both), 38, 39, 45
Art Directors & TRIP Photo Library: 16,
    19, 20, 21, 34, 44 (both)
Michelle Burgess: 30 (top)
Christine Osborne Pictures: 7, 8, 18, 25, 28,
    33, 43
Getty Images/Hulton Archive: 13, 37
Haga Library, Japan: cover, 35, 40
HBL Network Photo Agency: 3 (top), 5, 17,
    22, 31
I-Africa: 41
Illustrated London News Picture Library:
    12 (bottom)
International Photobank: 1, 6, 9 (both)
John R. Jones: 2, 3 (bottom), 10
Jason Lauré/Lauré Communications: 27, 29
Lauré Communications: 14
Lonely Planet Images: 23
Sylvia Cordaiy Photo Library: 12 (top)
Topham Picturepoint: 15, 36
Nik Wheeler: 4, 24

Digital Scanning by Superskill Graphics Pte Ltd

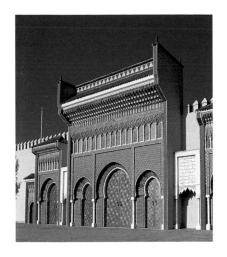

Contents

Words that appear in the glossary are printed in **boldface** type the first time they occur in the text.

Welcome to Morocco!

Although Morocco is located in Africa, its culture is a combination of African, European, and Arabic **traditions**. For centuries, the country has been ruled by kings, but since 1956, Morocco's kings have been trying to establish a more democratic form of government. Let's explore Morocco and learn about its people, history, and government.

Opposite: This young girl is wearing traditional Berber clothing and jewelry. Silver jewelry is a craft specialty of the Berber people.

Below: Camels are good transportation in the desert. They walk well in sand and can go a long time without water.

The Flag of Morocco

When it was adopted, in the 1600s, Morocco's flag was solid red. In 1915, French rulers added a green, five-pointed star. The star is called the Seal of Solomon. It is an ancient symbol that is believed to provide protection against evil.

The Land

Morocco occupies the northwestern corner of the African continent and has an area of 172,413 square miles (446,550 square kilometers). To the east and south, it shares its borders with Algeria and Mauritania. To the west and north, the Atlantic Ocean and the Mediterranean Sea separate the country from Portugal and Spain.

Below: Morocco's **diverse** landscape includes four major mountain ranges: the Rif, Middle Atlas, High Atlas, and Anti-Atlas.

Mountains, Deserts, and Rivers

Mountains and desert are Morocco's main geographic features. In the north, the Rif Mountains stretch east to west along the Mediterranean coast. The Middle Atlas, High Atlas, and Anti-Atlas mountain ranges extend north to south through the center of the country, separating coastal agricultural areas from the vast Sahara Desert. Rain and melting snow from the mountains feed rivers that **irrigate** farmland. Two of the most important rivers in Morocco are the Sebou and the Oum er-Rbia.

Above: This city is on the Oum er-Rbia River, which flows from the High Atlas Mountains to the Atlantic Ocean. Most of Morocco's cities are on either the Atlantic coast or the **fertile** plains along the country's main rivers.

Climate

Morocco can have a snowstorm in the mountains, mild weather on the coast, and extreme heat in the desert — all on the same day! Normally, however, summers are warm and dry, winters are cool and wet. Along the Atlantic coast, sea breezes keep temperatures **moderate**, except very far south, where it is hot and dry all year round. Central areas of the country are very warm, with summer heat that can be **stifling**.

Above: In spring, wildflowers thrive in the mild weather of the Moroccan countryside.

Plants and Animals

With its many different geographic areas, Morocco also has a wide variety of plants and animals. Eucalyptus and cork oak are among the types of trees growing in forests between the coast and the mountains. Cedar forests grow high in the mountains, and date palms are common on desert **oases**.

Forest wildlife includes lynx, foxes, and monkeys. The mountains are home to leopards and gazelles, while hyenas, antelope, and many kinds of reptiles and insects inhabit the deserts.

Above: Mountain goats are among the many kinds of animals that can be found in Morocco's hilly regions.

Left: Storks are one of many types of birds that spend each spring and autumn in Morocco as they travel back and forth between colder and warmer climates further north and south.

History

Humans may have lived in Morocco as long ago as 15,000 B.C. The Berbers, however, are the earliest inhabitants in recorded history. The Berbers already had well-established communities by the time **Phoenician** traders arrived in about 800 B.C. The Phoenicians settled mainly along the Mediterranean coast and by about 400 B.C., controlled all of northern Africa, including Morocco.

Below: Many of the buildings in North African cities are made of sun-baked earth and have support beams that are made from the wood of palm trees.

Roman Morocco

In 146 B.C., Roman armies destroyed the city of Carthage, which was the center of Phoenician power in North Africa. At first, the Romans just took control of Morocco's seaports and trade routes, but around A.D. 50, they started to form colonies. The Romans introduced new farming methods in Morocco, and the country soon became an important source of grain and olive oil for the Roman Empire.

Above: Although now in ruins, the city of Volubilis, in northern Morocco, was once a center of Roman culture.

The Berbers and Islam

Throughout Phoenician and Roman rule, the Berbers managed to hold on to their independence, living mainly in Morocco's mountain and desert areas. After the fall of the Roman Empire, in the fifth century, other invaders came to rule North Africa, but the Berbers held their ground. Arab invaders in the early 700s brought the Islam religion to Morocco. By the end of that century, the Berbers had defeated the Arabs but kept their religion.

Above: Melilla is one of two cities in Morocco that is still governed by Spain. The other Spanish city is Ceuta. Most of the people living in these cities are Spanish, but Melilla also has a large Berber community.

Left: This drawing shows Moroccans trying to protect their land against French intruders in the 1800s.

European Intruders

After defeating the Arabs, the Berber tribes united to form the first Moroccan **dynasty**. The country **flourished** until the shaky Marinid dynasty took power in 1269. As Morocco became weaker, European nations began to move in.

In the early 1500s, Portugal set up bases on the Mediterranean coast. Spain followed soon after. In 1912, after centuries of power struggles, the Treaty of Fez gave France control of Morocco's government.

Above: In 1955, Moroccans joyfully celebrated Sultan Mohammed Ben Youssef's return from **exile**. French officials forced the Moroccan leader out of the country in 1953 because he wanted to end French control over Morocco.

Independent Morocco

Moroccans resisted French control, especially after World War II (1939–1945) weakened it, and on March 2, 1956, Morocco declared independence. Sultan Mohammed Ben Youssef, who had been exiled by the French, returned to rule as King Mohammed V. When Mohammed V died, in 1961, his son, Hassan II, took the throne and ruled for almost forty years. Since 1999, King Hassan's son, Mohammed VI, has been Morocco's monarch.

Above:
Like his father, Mohammed V, Hassan II (*front*), tried to reform government and improve human rights. Because Morocco was so **unstable**, however, both kings ruled with strong control.

Moulay Idriss (?–A.D. 791)

Arab Muslim Moulay Idriss claimed to be a **descendant** of Islam's founder, the prophet Mohammed. His strong belief in Islam helped Idriss unite the Berbers, who were also Muslims, to start Morocco's first dynasty.

Moulay Ismail (1645–1727)

The first king of Morocco's current ruling dynasty, the Alaouites, Moulay Ismail gained control of all Morocco in the 1600s. He was also a powerful force against Europeans, driving the Spanish out of several colonies and the British out of Tangier.

Abd el-Krim (c. 1882–1963)

Tribal leader Abd el-Krim led Berber armies against the Spanish and the French in the 1920s. He was defeated in 1926 by a combined Spanish-French army. In 1958, King Mohammed V gave him the title National Hero.

Abd el-Krim

Government and the Economy

Officially, Morocco is a **constitutional monarchy**, but the monarch has almost complete control. The king chooses the country's prime minister, approves the **cabinet**, and decides **foreign policy**. He is also the highest-ranking religious leader and commander-in-chief of the military. The legislature of Morocco has elected members but limited power.

Below: Morocco's legislature is made up of the Chamber of Representatives and the Chamber of Counselors. The legislature meets in the Houses of Parliament (*below*), located in Rabat, which is Morocco's capital city.

Law and the Courts

The legal system in Morocco is based on both Islamic law and French and Spanish civil law. All Supreme Court judges must be recommended by the Supreme Council of the Judiciary, which is controlled by the king.

Local Governments

With sixteen administrative regions, Morocco has several levels of local government. The smallest units are known as *qaidates* (kah-EED-ates).

Above: The king's palace, in Rabat, is a magnificent display of Islamic architecture.

The Economy

Like most other developing countries, Morocco struggles with a high rate of **poverty**. The economy depends on agriculture, which employs nearly half of the country's workforce.

The largest industry in Morocco is phosphate mining, but tourism also helps the economy. About two million tourists visit Morocco each year. Other important industries include leather products and **textiles**, and Moroccan handicrafts are sold all over the world.

Above:
This equipment is part of a phosphate plant in Khouribga. Morocco is one of the world's largest producers of phosphate rock, which is a mineral used to make most kinds of fertilizers and many types of cleaning products.

Transportation

With Morocco's good road, railroad, and bus systems, traveling is easy. In the crowded cities, however, people often use bicycles or motor scooters instead of cars or buses to get around.

For travel into and out of Morocco, the national airline, Royal Air Maroc, offers flights to thirty-seven countries, including the United States. Morocco also has ten seaports that are used by both large ships and passenger ferries.

Below: The main entry point for most visitors to Morocco is the Mohammed V Airport, which is in Casablanca.

People and Lifestyle

Berbers and Arabs are Morocco's main **ethnic** groups. Signs of the early Berber culture date back about four thousand years. Some Arab groups first came to Morocco in the seventh century, as invaders. Other Arabs were Muslims driven out of Spain, a mainly Catholic country, in the 1400s.

Smaller ethnic groups in Morocco include black Africans, Jews, and Saharawis, who are wandering tribes that live in the Western Sahara area.

Below: Many people in Casablanca and other large cities in Morocco have no choice but to live in run-down, unsafe housing because they have not been able to find jobs.

Struggling Against Poverty

For centuries, Morocco's Berbers lived in mountain villages. Now, many of them live in cities. Half of the people in Morocco today live in cities. Since the country gained independence, most Moroccans, especially in **rural** areas, have been struggling to make a living. Many have moved from small villages to large cities, hoping to find jobs and a better life. Instead, they have found overcrowding, a lack of housing, and poor health care.

Above: A high birth rate in Morocco has resulted in a very young population. About 60 percent of the country's people are under the age of twenty-five.

Family Life

Because many generations often live together, the families in Morocco can become very large. Extra rooms may even be added to a house to make sure that everyone has enough space when children get married and have their own children. Young adults who move away from rural villages to find jobs in the cities are expected to send money home to support their families.

Above: In Morocco, meals are important family occasions. To make room for large families at mealtimes, people usually sit on the floor, surrounding food placed in the center of the floor.

Marriage in Morocco

A traditional Moroccan wedding lasts several days, and the entire families of both the bride and the groom are involved in the celebration. Marriages in Morocco are often arranged by the couple's parents. Sometimes, the bride and groom do not meet each other until their wedding day. Today, however, many traditional customs are changing.

Below: Traditional Moroccan marriage customs will most likely change a lot by the time these boys grow up. Even now, especially in the cities, young men choose their own wives, and couples are dating before they marry.

Education

Before Morocco became independent, foreign rulers did not think Moroccans needed to be educated. So, today, less than half of the population over age fifteen can read and write. Independent Morocco spends a large portion of its national budget building schools and hiring teachers. It is trying very hard both to improve the country's school system and to meet a **literacy** goal of 80 percent by the year 2010.

Below: Morocco's laws require that all children ages seven to thirteen go to school, but because the country does not have enough school buildings or teachers, only about 70 percent of these children can attend.

Children in Morocco must complete six years of basic education. After that, they may choose to attend a secondary school, but secondary education is not required. Secondary school lasts three years, during which students focus on either general or technical course work.

At both basic and secondary levels of education, classes are taught in the Arabic language, but all students learn French, too. In secondary school, many students also learn English.

Above:
Fez University is one of twenty-seven schools of higher learning in Morocco, thirteen of which are universities. A student must have a diploma from a secondary school before he or she can continue on to higher education.

Religion

Almost all of the Moroccan people are Muslims. Only about 2 percent belong to other religions, and they are mainly Jews and Christians.

Muslims are members of the Islam religion, which started on the Arabian Peninsula in the seventh century. Islam spread quickly through the Middle East to northern Africa. Morocco has been an Islamic country since the late 700s.

Mohammed and Islam

Like Jews and Christians, Muslims believe in one God. Muslims call God "Allah." Many of the prophets honored by Jews and Christians, such as Moses, Abraham, and Jesus, are also honored by Muslims. Islam's most important prophet, however, is Mohammed.

Islam was founded by the prophet Mohammed, to whom God revealed the truths and teachings of the religion. Mohammed wrote God's teachings in a book called the Qur'an, which is still the holy book of the Islam religion.

Left:
Five times a day, religious officials call Muslims to prayer by chanting "*Allahu akbar*" (ah-LAH-who AHK-bar), which means "God is great." The call to prayer traditionally began by blowing a horn, but, today, most mosques use loudspeakers.

Language

Arabic is Morocco's official language. It is also the language of the Qur'an. Used throughout the Middle East and the Arabian Peninsula, as well as in North Africa, spoken Arabic has many variations. Written Arabic, however, is the same everywhere.

In Morocco, spoken Arabic includes many French words, which reflects the country's history of control by France. Millions of Berbers in Morocco still speak three main versions of their own language, but they also speak Arabic.

Left: Street signs in Morocco include both Arabic and French languages. Even Moroccans without very much education are able to speak basic French. Educated Moroccans speak a mixed version of Arabic and French, often using both languages in the same sentence.

Literature

Until about the 1940s, the literature of Morocco was mainly poetry and storytelling, which had long been a Berber tradition. During the struggle for independence, and even after independence, the country's social and political problems became the subjects of most Moroccan literature. Because works on these topics were often **banned** by the king, many writers left Morocco to live in France, where they could write more freely.

Above: Magazines and newspapers in both the Arabic and French languages are readily available in Morocco. Many Moroccans read one of these languages as easily as the other. Moroccan authors, however, usually write only in French.

Handicrafts

The folk art and crafts of Morocco are known around the world for their high quality. Berber weavers make rugs and carpets in colors and designs that are unique to each tribe. The pottery from each region of the country also has a unique style. Both Berbers and Jews design exquisite jewelry, and many of their masterpieces are displayed in Morocco's museums. Morocco is also famous for its leather products.

Museums

Morocco has a variety of both art and archaeological museums. Some of the country's ancient palaces have been turned into showcases for traditional art. The Museum of Contemporary Art, in Tangier, displays the work of Morocco's modern artists. A large public museum in Rabat has exhibits of **artifacts** that date back to the Stone Age, while Dar Batha Museum in Fez has historical carpets and ceramics.

Below: Moroccan handicrafts used in everyday life are featured at the Museum of Arts and Crafts, in Tetouan.

Leisure

Most people in Morocco, especially women, spend their leisure time with their families, visiting other families, sharing meals, and celebrating family events. Family activities away from home might include a trip to a city park or to the beach. For men, cities offer modern kinds of entertainment such as movie theaters and discos.

Below: Even in the cities, Moroccan women are not as free as men to take part in activities outside the family. Although they still honor most Islamic traditions, some women now wear Western clothing and leave their hair uncovered.

In farming areas, people are usually working too hard to have much leisure time, but they make time to celebrate family events and religious holidays, sometimes with music and dancing.

Besides being included in all family activities, Moroccan children have other traditional pastimes. Young girls learn to keep house, while boys, who have more freedom, like to play soccer.

Above:
Men in Morocco like to meet friends at neighborhood cafés for coffee or tea and conversation. Men have more freedom than women to go to cafés or movies or to enjoy other types of entertainment that Moroccan cities have to offer.

Sports

Moroccans of all ages love soccer, and their national team, known as the Lions of the Atlas, has long been one of the best in Africa. In 1970, the Lions of the Atlas became the first team from Africa ever to reach the final rounds of World Cup competition. In the 1986 World Cup event, the Lions became the first African or Arab team ever to move into the round of sixteen finalists.

Below: Moroccan goalkeeper Driss Benzakri (*right*) was unable to block a goal-scoring kick made by Michael Owen (*far left*) in a match against England during the 1998 King Hassan II International Cup competition.

Left: In 1999, Morocco's best known international athlete, Hicham al-Guerrouj (*right*), set the current world record in the 1-mile (1.6-km) run. Al-Guerrouj also holds the record for the 1,500-meter run.

Track and field is Morocco's second most popular sport. In 1984, at the Los Angeles Olympics, Moroccan athlete Nawal al-Moutawakil became the first Arab woman to win a gold medal in the 400-meter hurdles event.

Festivals and Holidays

Ramadan is Islam's holiest month and its most important religious festival. As in all Islamic countries, the Muslims in Morocco celebrate by fasting, which means not eating or drinking anything during daylight hours. A sunset meal called *iftar* (if-TAR) breaks the fast and brings families together each evening to pray. The four- to five-day holiday known as *Eid al-fitr* (eed al-FIT-er) celebrates the end of Ramadan fasting.

Above: For the three-day Islamic holiday *Eid al-adha* (eed al-AHD-hah), farmers in Morocco sell their sheep to Muslims who still follow the tradition of killing sheep as a sacrifice to God. This holiday honors the ancient prophet Abraham, who was willing to sacrifice his only son, Isaac, as proof of his devotion to God.

Other Muslim holidays in Morocco include the Islamic New Year and the birthday of the prophet Mohammed.

The Berbers have festivals, too, to honor some of the holy men of their culture. Celebrations typically combine prayer, music, and dancing. The most important Berber festival honors the country's first king, Moulay Idriss. The festival is held in a village of the same name, where the king's tomb is located.

Below:
One of Morocco's most interesting celebrations is a marriage festival held each year in the Middle Atlas Mountains. During this colorful and lively three-day event, women can choose husbands.

Food

Moroccan food is a blend of traditional Berber cooking and Arab spices, such as cinnamon, cardamom, and nutmeg, usually flavored with olive oil and lemon or orange peel.

A typical main dish includes steamy hot couscous and cooked vegetables. Couscous is a grain made of cracked wheat. Meats such as chicken, pigeon, or lamb might also be served, and seafood is a popular addition along the coasts. For special feasts, Moroccans may roast a whole lamb over charcoal.

Left: A stew called *tagine* (tah-JEEN) is a favorite dish of many Moroccans. Tagine is made of spiced meat and vegetables.

No Moroccan meal is complete without *harissa* (hah-REE-sah), which is a sauce made with oil, garlic, and hot peppers. Because harissa is very hot, it is served separately so that diners can use as much or as little as they wish.

Desserts in Morocco are usually either fresh fruit and nuts or pastries made with almond paste. Mint tea, which is the country's national drink, is served at the end of every meal. Coffee is another very popular drink.

Above:
Most Moroccans eat their meals at home, but, in the cities, people sometimes stop for a meal or a snack at an outdoor food stall. Roast chicken, lamb kabobs, and *kafta* (KAHF-tah), which is lamb rolled up in flat bread, are commonly available at outdoor stalls.

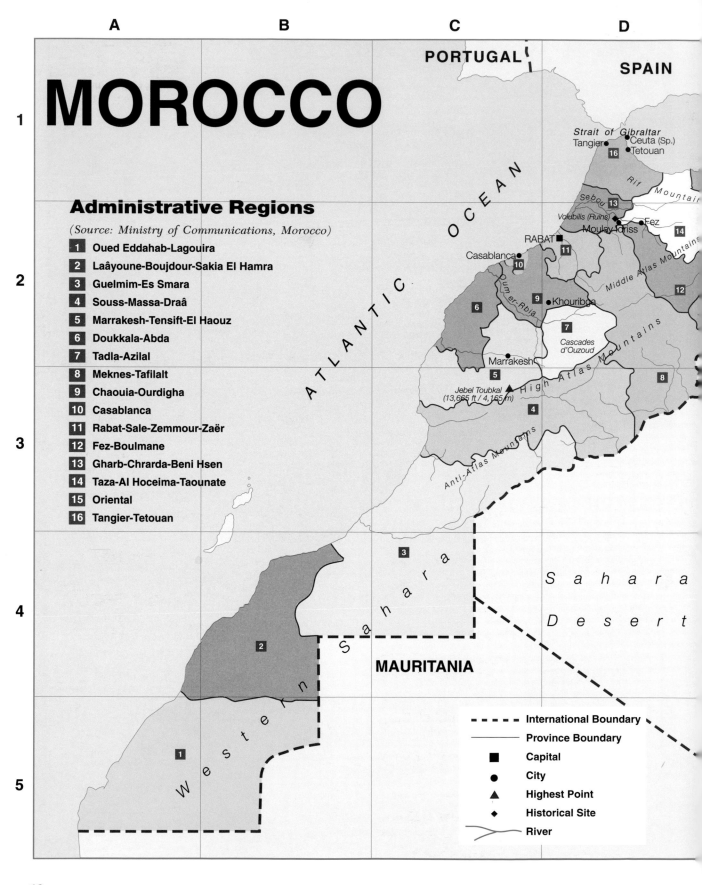

MOROCCO

PORTUGAL

SPAIN

Administrative Regions

(Source: Ministry of Communications, Morocco)

1. Oued Eddahab-Lagouira
2. Laâyoune-Boujdour-Sakia El Hamra
3. Guelmim-Es Smara
4. Souss-Massa-Draâ
5. Marrakesh-Tensift-El Haouz
6. Doukkala-Abda
7. Tadla-Azilal
8. Meknes-Tafilalt
9. Chaouia-Ourdigha
10. Casablanca
11. Rabat-Sale-Zemmour-Zaër
12. Fez-Boulmane
13. Gharb-Chrarda-Beni Hsen
14. Taza-Al Hoceima-Taounate
15. Oriental
16. Tangier-Tetouan

Strait of Gibraltar
Tangier
Ceuta (Sp.)
Tetouan
Rif Mountains
Sebou
Volubilis (Ruins)
Moulay Idriss
Fez
Casablanca
RABAT
Oum er-Rbia
Khouribga
Cascades d'Ouzoud
Middle Atlas Mountains
Marrakesh
Jebel Toubkal
(13,665 ft / 4,165 m)
High Atlas Mountains
Anti-Atlas Mountains

ATLANTIC OCEAN

Western Sahara

Sahara Desert

MAURITANIA

- - - International Boundary
— Province Boundary
■ Capital
● City
▲ Highest Point
◆ Historical Site
〜 River

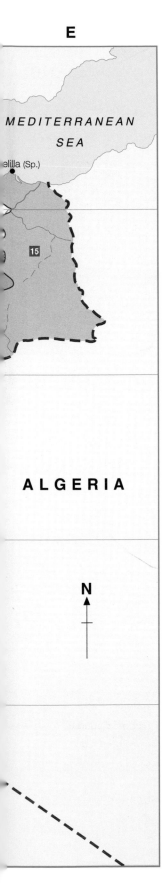

MEDITERRANEAN
SEA

elilla (Sp.)

15

ALGERIA

N

Above: Moroccan markets sell a variety of dried foods and spices.

Algeria C4–E1
Anti-Atlas
    Mountains C3
Atlantic Ocean
    A5–D1

Casablanca C2
Cascades
    d'Ouzoud D2
Ceuta D1

Fez D2

High Atlas Mountains
    C3–D2

Jebel Toubkal C3

Khouribga D2

Marrakesh C2
Mauritania B4–E5
Mediterranean
    Sea D1–E1

Melilla E1
Middle Atlas
    Mountains D2
Moulay Idriss D2

Oum er-Rbia
    River C2

Portugal C1

Rabat D2
Rif Mountains D1

Sahara Desert
    C4–E4

Sebou River D1–D2
Spain C1–E1
Strait of
    Gibraltar D1

Tangier D1
Tetouan D1

Volubilis D2

Western Sahara
    A5–C4

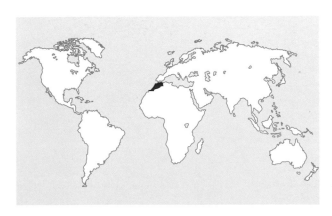

Quick Facts

Official Name   Kingdom of Morocco

Capital   Rabat

Official Language   Arabic

Population   31,167,783 (2003 estimate)

Land Area   172,413 square miles (446,550 square km)

Highest Point   Jebel Toubkal 13,665 feet (4,165 m)

Main Religion   Islam

Holidays   New Year's Day (January 1)

Independence Manifesto Day (January 11)

Labor Day (May 1)

National Day (July 30)

Reunification Day (August 14)

King's and People's Revolution Day (August 20)

Anniversary of the Green March (November 6)

Independence Day (November 18)

Currency   Moroccan Dirham (9.47400 MAD = U.S. $1 as of 2003)

Opposite: The Cascades d'Ouzoud waterfall, in central Morocco, drops 328 feet (100 m).

Glossary

artifacts: simple objects, such as tools, that were made by people and have historical or cultural importance.

banned: forbidden or considered illegal.

cabinet: a special group of advisors who help the leader of a country manage the government.

calligraphy: the art of elaborate and elegant handwriting or lettering, which is often used for decorative purposes.

constitutional monarchy: a type of government that is led by a king or a queen but is ruled according to the laws of an established constitution.

descendant: a person from a recent generation who was born into a particular family of ancestors.

diverse: having many differences and much variety.

dynasty: a series of rulers over a long period who belong to the same family.

ethnic: related to a particular race or culture of people.

exile (n): the state of being sent away by force from a person's homeland.

fertile: able to produce new life.

flourished: grew or developed quickly and successfully.

foreign policy: a government's plans or principles that determine how the country acts toward other countries.

immigrants: people who move away from their homeland to settle in another country.

irrigate: to supply water to dry areas of land for the purpose of growing crops.

literacy: the ability to read and write.

moderate: not extreme in any way.

oases: fertile areas in a desert region that have a source of water.

Phoenician: belonging to a great ancient civilization of traders and explorers who were among the first to colonize the Mediterranean Sea area.

poverty: the state of not having enough money and living necessities, such as food, clothing, and shelter.

rural: related to the countryside.

stifling: suffocating.

textiles: woven fabrics or cloth.

traditions: customs and practices passed down from one generation to another.

unique: special, often one of a kind.

unstable: not firm, steady, or strong.

More Books to Read

Ali: Child of the Desert. Jonathan London (Lothrop Lee & Shepard)

The Children of Morocco. The World's Children series. Jules Hermes (Carolrhoda Books)

Morocco. Countries series. Bob Italia (Abdo)

Morocco. Countries: Faces and Places series. Patrick Merrick (Child's World)

Morocco in Pictures. Visual Geography series. Noel Sheridan, editor (Lerner Publications)

North Africa: Morocco. Ancient and Living Cultures series. Mira Bartok, Christine Ronan, and Esther Grisham (Goodyear)

The Sahara Desert. Great Record Breakers in Nature series. Aileen Weintraub (PowerKids Press)

Zorah's Magic Carpet. Stefan Czernecki (Hyperion)

Videos

Africa. World's Most Exotic Places series. (Marathon Music & Video)

The Pilot Guide to Morocco. Globe Trekker series. (555 Productions)

Saharawi: The Men of the Desert. People & Places of Africa series. (Library Video)

Web Sites

geogweb.berkeley.edu/GeoImages/ Miller/millerone.html

www.mapzones.com/world/africa/ morocco/introindex.php

www.peacecorps.gov/kids/world/ europemed/morocco.html

www.worldtrek.org/odyssey/africa/ kidstimemorocco.html

Due to the dynamic nature of the Internet, some web sites stay current longer than others. To find additional web sites, use a reliable search engine with one or more of the following keywords to help you locate information about Morocco. Keywords: *Berbers, Casablanca, Jebel Toubkal, Marrakesh, Sahara Desert, tagine, Volubilis.*

Index